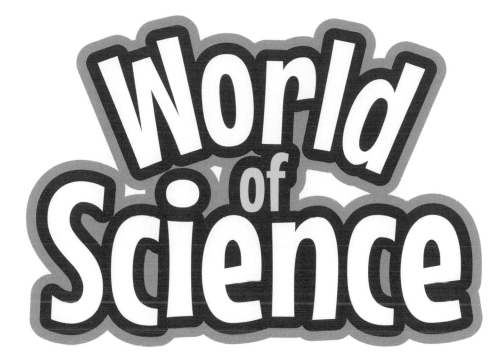

World of Science

Adventures with Useful Plants and Fungi

Edited by

Karen Kwek and Kathy Wong

WS Education

NEW JERSEY · LONDON · SINGAPORE · BEIJING · SHANGHAI · HONG KONG · TAIPEI · CHENNAI · TOKYO

Published by

WS Education, an imprint of

World Scientific Publishing Co. Pte. Ltd.

5 Toh Tuck Link, Singapore 596224

USA office: 27 Warren Street, Suite 401-402, Hackensack, NJ 07601

UK office: 57 Shelton Street, Covent Garden, London WC2H 9HE

National Library Board, Singapore Cataloguing in Publication Data
Name(s): Kwek, Karen, editor. | Wong, Kathy, editor.
Title: Adventures with useful plants and fungi / edited by Karen Kwek and Kathy Wong.
Other Title(s): World of science comics.
Description: Singapore : WS Education, [2022]
Identifier(s): ISBN 978-981-12-6263-0 (hardcover) | 978-981-12-6264-7 (paperback) |
    978-981-12-6265-4 (ebook for institutions) | 978-981-12-6266-1 (ebook for individuals)
Subject(s): LCSH: Plants, Useful--Comic books, strips, etc. | Plants, Useful--Juvenile literature. |
    Fungi--Comic books, strips, etc. | Fungi--Juvenile literature. | Graphic novels.
Classification: DDC 581.6--dc23

British Library Cataloguing-in-Publication Data
A catalogue record for this book is available from the British Library.

Published by arrangement by ENGLISH CORNER PUBLISHING PTE LTD

Design and layout by Loo Chuan Ming

Printed in Singapore

What are plants?
And what are fungi?

If you thought of trees and shrubs as examples of plants, and mushrooms and mould as examples of fungi, you're on the right track! Our world has a huge variety of plants and fungi, and many of them provide us with food, medicine and building materials.

What is the world's smallest flowering plant? Which plant can calm our nerves? How do we get leather from mushrooms? Stroll through the purple lavender fields. Search the forest for reishi mushrooms. From tropical forests to open fields, get ready to be wowed by some useful plants and fungi!

A Guide to Experiencing the Bonus Features in this Book

See a QR code? Scan it to access bonus resources!

Contents

Turning Over A New Leaf

Deciduous and Evergreen Plants

Plants may be classified as evergreen or deciduous. An evergreen plant is green throughout the year. A deciduous plant loses its leaves as the seasons change in a process called abscission.

Surviving Winter

Being deciduous has its advantages and disadvantages. When deciduous plants lose their leaves, they can conserve energy and nutrients, and survive in cold and dry climates. However, they need even more resources (water and air) to grow back their leaves in the next season.

Yes. It is one of the characteristics of evergreen leaves. The leaf surface area is small and waxy, and water from the leaves doesn't evaporate easily.

Henry, have I answered your question? Shall we continue our work?

Hee, hee… Yes, Uncle Thomas!

So that's why the Thuja 'evergreen giant' doesn't wither due to a lack of water and can survive during winter.

Hee, hee… It is revenge time!

Urgh! Splat!

Ha ha…I knew what you were thinking!

Ahhh!...

9

Leaf Me Alone

The leaves of evergreen plants are often scale-like or needle-like in cone-bearing trees. Some plants, like the Dieffenbachia, have broad, waxy leaves.

Evergreen Plants

Pines

There are many pine species such as red pines, black pines and eastern white pines. Each evergreen pine has its own characteristics. For example, red pines have brown-red bark.

The bark and leaves of a Japanese red pine

Norway Spruce

The Norway spruce is a large, fast-growing evergreen conifer that is widely planted and often used as a Christmas tree.

Douglas Fir

Douglas firs can be 50 to 80 feet tall. Due to its strength, the douglas fir is used primarily in building and construction.

A Birthday Bouquet

Flowering Fragrance

Fruit trees and vegetables are flowering plants. Flowers come in many colours and some give off a nice fragrance.

A Birthday Bouquet

Types of Non-Flowering Plants

There are two groups of non-flowering plants — those that reproduce by seeds (gymnosperms such as conifers) and those that reproduce by spores (ferns and mosses). The spores of a fern may be found on the underside of its leaves.

Are there plants in this world that do not flower?

Of course there are. Plants are divided into flowering and non-flowering types.

I see. Which are the plants that do not flower?

Ferns and mosses are plants that do not flower.

Where can we find these plants?

These plants usually grow in dark and humid places.

Come, let's go and find some!

Brother, are these non-flowering plants?

Yes. These are ferns.

seeds

Reproduction of Flowering Plants

Most flowering plants reproduce by seeds. Some use asexual vegetative propagation and grow new plants from rhizomes (ginger plant) or tubers (potato).

We can pair ferns with flowers to form a really nice bouquet. Let's take this and that...

Enough, you're over-doing it!

On Mother Raccoon's birthday...

Mum, happy birthday!

Thank you for your blessings!

Mum, we made you a special bouquet.

Thank you! How very thoughtful of you!

Of course, I do.

Do you like our gift, Mum?

Mum approves. I am so happy!

There you go again!

Ha ha ha!

An Ancient Plant

There are about 10,500 known species of ferns and they outnumber the other types of non-flowering plants. Based on fossil records, scientists believe that ferns already existed on Earth 360 million years ago. However, most of the earliest ferns have gone extinct.

15

A Birthday Bouquet

Pin-Sized Plants

A Tiny Plant

Watermeal plants grow in ponds and paddy fields. They have no roots or leaves. A watermeal plant is shaped like a ball that is about 1.3 to 1.5 millimetres long. Its width is no more than one millimetre.

Pros and Cons

Watermeal plants are rich in nutrients such as protein. Some farmers use the plants as forage to feed their geese and ducks. Because of their strong reproductive ability, they can quickly cover an entire pond surface when growing conditions are ideal. This cover can block sunlight from reaching plants in the water. Affected plants will die and decay, reducing the amount of dissolved oxygen in the pond water.

Pin-Sized Plants

World-Record Holder

The very tiny watermeal holds three world records: it is the world's smallest flowering plant, it has the smallest flower in the world and it has the smallest fruit in the world as well.

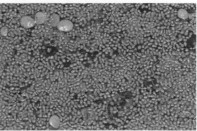

WATERMEAL

The structure of the watermeal is simple. Its roots, stem and leaves have all degenerated. Its interior is full of small gas-filled chambers that are mainly made up of parenchyma cells used to perform photosynthesis.

20

Watermeal plants grow and reproduce quickly. Their main mode of reproduction is asexual, which is very rapid. A new plant can grow in about 30 to 36 hours.

Watermeal plants can grow among other aquatic plants or other types of duckweed. There can be as many as a million watermeal plants in every square metre of water.

Radical Roots

A Coastal Plant

Mangroves grow in tropical regions and coastal intertidal zones. Mangroves are also a plant community that is composed of salt-tolerant plants.

This is a mangrove plant. These criss-crossing branches are its prop roots.

Why does it have so many prop roots?

Mangrove plants grow on soft soil. They need their prop roots for support.

My prop roots go down deep into the soil and establish a firm hold that allows me to be firmly fixed in the soft soil.

I see.

Let's go and check out the mangroves!

Mangroves are extremely important to the coastal ecosystems they inhabit.

These prop roots are spectacular!

Mangroves have well-developed roots that grow firmly in the beach sand. They protect shorelines from damaging winds, waves and floods.

Rooted and Grounded

Apart from prop roots, mangrove trees have other types of roots such as buttress roots and pneumatophores. Buttress roots help to stabilise the trees in the soft mud. Pneumatophores extend out from the mud to take in oxygen from the air.

Buttress roots   *Pneumatophores*

Wow, so mangroves are very important! If there is a tsunami, mangroves may at least reduce the disaster.

But in recent years, mangroves have been destroyed due to mariculture development, reclamation of agricultural land and all kinds of construction projects.

That's true.

The mangrove forest area is gradually decreasing.

What should we do then?

Luckily, people now understand the importance of mangroves, and are beginning to maintain and reconstruct the mangrove forests.

I want to help save the mangroves.

Yes, we will do it together!

Let's go back. There should be someone here to pick us up now!

Okay!

Hidden by the Tide

Mangroves have to tolerate tidal changes. During high tide, mangrove roots are covered by seawater and only their tree crown sticks above the water surface. The whole trees can only be seen at low tide.

Ahhh...

Thump!

Manny, are you okay?

Yes, I'm okay!

Ouch! My foot!

Ouch... Ouch...

Hee hee, it was a fiddler crab!

25

Fiddler Crabs

Fiddler crabs are commonly seen in mangrove forests. They have protruding eyes that look like matchsticks. Male fiddler crabs have a large and a small claw, while the females have two small claws.

The Roles Of Mangroves

Apart from protecting shorelines and preventing erosion, mangroves provide many living organisms with a nutrient-rich environment. Thus, many animals such as birds, fish, shrimp, crabs and shellfish are drawn to live and breed there.

Mangroves also serve as natural sewage treatment systems that filter organic material or toxic heavy metals that come from rivers and oceans.

Today, mangrove forests are sites for eco-tourism. This allows visitors to learn about the importance of mangroves from the locals themselves. In this way, the local communities gain a sustainable livelihood and the mangrove forests are conserved.

26

Radical Roots

The "Berry" Inedible Tree

The "Berry" Inedible Tree

A Deciduous Tree

The chinaberry tree is a deciduous tree that grows up to 15 feet tall. Its bark is dark brown or grey-brown, with deep irregular cracks.

General Habitat

Chinaberry trees are native to India, Southeast Asia and northern Australia, but are now widely distributed in the tropical and subtropical regions of Asia. They can also be grown in temperate regions.

The "Berry" Inedible Tree

Uncle Billy's house...

There's a citrus long-horned beetle here.

Wow! It's huge!

Huh?

The chinaberry tree is the host plant for citrus long-horned beetles. The beetles like to eat the bark, tender twigs and leaves of the chinaberry tree. They also lay their eggs inside the bark.

I see!

I've just dug up some sweet potatoes. I can steam them for you.

Awesome!

Not Very Fussy
Chinaberry trees grow well in neutral, acid and sandy soils, and limestone areas. They like warm and humid weather. Mature chinaberry trees are resistant to drought.

Shade from the Sun

Chinaberry trees bloom in the spring. Their flowers are pink or lavender, star-shaped and have a fragrant smell. Thus, chinaberry trees are seen as ornamental trees. Their large spreading canopies also make them good shade trees.

Chinaberry wood is light, soft and lustrous. It has a rough but beautiful texture. It can be made into furniture, models, agricultural tools and musical instruments.

Does the chinaberry tree have any other uses?

The chinaberry's flowers can be steamed to extract essential oil. The pulp and skin of the fruit can be made into white wine and industrial alcohol.

Wow, the chinaberry tree has so many uses!

Puh!

That stinks!

Ha ha, sorry! I ate too many sweet potatoes…

Ha ha ha!

The "Berry" Inedible Tree

Beware!
The bark, leaves, flowers and berries of the Chinaberry are all toxic to humans and some mammals including cats and dogs. Cattle and some birds are able to consume the berries without being harmed. Some symptoms of poisoning from Chinaberry include diarrhoea, vomiting, loss of appetite, weakness and cardiac arrest.

Chinaberry Tree

Chinaberry trees are seasonal plants. In the spring, their new green buds emerge and their purple flowers bloom. When the flowers wither, the leaves turn dark green. The fruit hang on the withered branches. The fruit of a Chinaberry tree are drupes that are shaped like an egg or a ball. The unripe fruit appear green and turn light yellow, orange-yellow or yellow-brown when they are ripe.

The chinaberry tree is shaped like an umbrella and has pinnately compound leaves. The tree grows rapidly with a beautifully shaped crown. It is often grown as an ornamental shade tree.

Toosendanin can be extracted from chinaberry bark and made into a safe and effective insecticide against a hundred types of pests, several leaf fleas and nematodes.

Fields of Colour

Distribution of Lupins

Lupins can grow up to 70 centimetres tall and are mainly distributed in the west of North America, the Mediterranean region and Africa.

Lupin flowers can be in many colours including blue, purple, white and pink.

Can these flowers be grown as potted plants?

They can! As long as you water and fertilise them, they can be beautiful indoor potted plants.

Lupin stems and leaves can be used for grazing. They're excellent silage and can be fed to pigs and cows.

We should grow some lupins around our house for our pigs to eat.

Hey!

Blooming Season

Lupins bloom from March to May and bear fruit from April to July. They have a long blooming season and can be grown in large quantities. The flowers can be red, blue, pink, white, purple and cream.

Fields of Colour

Sunshine Lovers

Lupins are resistant to cold. They like a cool climate and places with plenty of sunshine. Lupins grow well in fertile, well-drained and sandy soil.

Fields of Colour

A Nutritious Snack
Lupin beans or seeds are egg-shaped, yellow, flat and smooth. They are rich in protein, dietary fibre and essential nutrients.

A Useful Ingredient

Lupin seeds can be added to food like salads. They can also be ground into flour and used for baking. However, for certain lupin species, the seeds must first be processed to remove the toxic compounds.

Lupin

Lupin plants have deep green leaves and colourful flower spikes. This makes them popular for use in landscaping. The Texas bluebonnet is one of the most popular ornamental lupins in the United States.

Fields of Colour

The name "lupin" comes from a Latin word that means "wolf". This was due to a mistaken belief that lupins soaked up, or "wolfed", minerals from the soil. However, we now know that lupins improve soil by adding nitrogen to it.

Lupins can be grown as a green manure to fertilise soil. In Canada, they are used as a cover crop for reforestation.

Royally Radiant

Royally Radiant

The next day...

The royal poinciana is an evergreen tree that is shaped like a broad umbrella.

Why haven't we seen any umbrella-shaped trees yet?

Look! Over there!

That must be a royal poinciana tree.

It looks just like a huge umbrella!

Wow, it's so tall!

An Ornamental Tree

Royal poinciana trees are found in many tropical and subtropical regions. During the blooming season, these trees are full of bright, red flowers. They have become a popular ornamental tree species.

The royal poinciana tree is pretty tall. It can grow up to more than 20 metres in height.

The tree is full of red flowers. They're so beautiful!

Adorned with green leaves and red flowers, the royal poinciana tree is considered the most brightly coloured tree species.

It's the national flower of the Republic of Madagascar and the city flower of China's Shantou.

It has spectacular roots too.

In order to adapt to the rainy climate, royal poinciana trees have plate-like roots that help them stand firmly in the ground.

I see!

43

Royally Radiant

Royal Poinciana Flowers

The flowers of the royal poinciana have five petals. Four are similar in size and red while the fifth is slightly larger with a red and white colouration. Yellow varieties also exist.

The leaves look pretty special! They have lots of tiny blades.

Its leaves are opposite.

Right. A royal poinciana tree leaf is a pinna that is made up of more than 100 leaflets. A larger pinnately compound leaf will be composed of more than ten pairs of pinnae.

There's an insect!

Bernard, throw away that leaf!

Useful Tree Bark

The bark of the royal poinciana is grey and smooth. It has medicinal properties and has been used for its anti-diabetic and anti-inflammatory effects. The wood of the tree is light and appears white or yellowish.

Dylan, what was that insect?

It was the caterpillar of a noctuid moth.

Is it eating the leaf?

Yes. Noctuid moths live on leaves. So they eat the royal poinciana leaves.

I can't let it continue to destroy the beautiful royal poinciana tree!

Don't touch it! Its stinging hairs have toxic substances; it's safer for us to keep away.

45

Royally Radiant

Living in Sunshine

The royal poinciana tree is a tropical tree species that flowers after growing for 6 to 8 years. It likes sunny, warm and humid environments. The optimal temperature for the tree is between 20 and 30 degrees Celsius.

Is it angry?

Hoo! I thought it was going to attack us. It scared me!

A few days later...

Ding dong!

Sign here, please.

Wow!

I saw how much you loved the royal poinciana tree, so I bought a potted one. You'll have to take good care of it.

No problem!

Beautiful but Deadly

The seeds and flowers of the royal poinciana tree are toxic. Accidental ingestion may result in dizziness, abdominal pain and diarrhoea.

Royal Poinciana Tree

The crown of the royal poinciana tree extends horizontally and hangs downwards, making it resemble an umbrella. With a rather dense crown, the royal poinciana tree provides a lot of shade.

As shade trees, royal poinciana trees create a microclimate effect that can lower the temperature and increase humidity. They are ornamental trees that can beautify the environment. However, it is important to prune the trees as the branches are prone to breaking in strong winds.

After a royal poinciana tree flowers, it produces seed pods that can grow up to 60 centimetres. As the seed pod ripens, it turns from green to dark brown. There are 40 to 50 small seeds hidden inside.

47

Cosmetics from Nature

Cosmetics from Nature

The Lipstick Tree

Achiote is a shrub or small tree originating from tropical regions of North, Central and South America. Native Americans originally used the seeds to make red body paint and lipstick. For this reason, the achiote is sometimes called the lipstick tree.

The Origin of Annatto

The pulp around the seeds is edible. It tastes similar to fresh pepper, with a hint of nutmeg sweetness. It is used to make annatto, a food colouring that gives a yellow to orange-red colour. Annatto is also added to dishes for flavour enhancement.

Many Uses

Annatto can be used in cosmetics such as nail gloss and soap. It is also used in household products such as floor wax, furniture polish and shoe polish. In some regions, it is also used as a dye for fabrics.

ACHIOTE TREE

The achiote tree is a small deciduous tree or shrub. Its leaves are heart-shaped and its flowers grow on the tips of its branches. The five petals of the flowers are pinkish-purple.

Achiote fruit are bright red capsules. When they ripen, they turn brown or reddish-brown. Their shells are covered in hard, short spines. When the fruit is fully ripe, it cracks open to expose the dark red seeds inside.

The reddish pulp covering the achiote seeds contains annatto, which is an edible natural pigment that is often used to colour cheese, cakes or desserts.

Annatto Cheese Coloring

Heat   Add   Enjoy

NEW ENGLAND
Cheesemaking
SUPPLY COMPANY
2 fl. oz. Store in a cool place away from direct sunlight

Cosmetics from Nature

Buzz Off, Mozzies!

Phew! Uncle Thomas, can we rest here? We've been walking for more than an hour.

Yeah, I'm tired too!

Just a little further... There's a place to rest up ahead.

There are lots of mosquitoes at the rest point...

Ahh...

Glug, glug...

Glug, glug...

Hzzzzz....

Hzzzzz....

Hzzzzz....

Hzzzzz....

Ah... there are so many mosquitoes!

Hzzzzz...

Hzzzzz...

Eee... I'm so itchy!

Let me get the mosquito repellent.

Buzz Off, Mozzies!

Natural Insect Repellents
Lemon balm is a lemon-scented herb from the mint family. It can be mixed with lavender flowers, mint, citronella, catnip and lemon grass to enhance mosquito-repelling effects.

Keep Insects Away!

In order to repel mosquitoes or insects effectively, spray on lemon balm repellent every hour. It can be continuously used for 6 to 9 months, if it is properly stored.

Catnip Plant

Catnip is a member of the mint family. It is a better mosquito repellent than DEET. Apart from repelling mosquitoes, it can also repel flies and cockroaches. Catnip and lemon balm work in the same way.

Plants That Repel Mosquitoes

Citronella Grass

The leaves of citronella grass produce an oil known as citronella which can be found in insect repellents and candles. Citronella grass is a perennial grass that grows to about 2.5 metres tall.

Mint

Mint plants are herbs from the genus Mentha. The fresh smell of mint is a natural insecticide and can also be used to remove odours. Mint can be rubbed over a bite to relieve itching.

Marigold

Marigold contains a compound known as pyrethrin which is used in insect repellents. Marigold flowers are edible and can be used as ornaments.

Lavender's Purple (Dilly Dilly)...

Lavender's Purple (Dilly Dilly)...

World-Famous Fields

Provence, in the South of France, is one of the world's most famous places to see lavender flowers. The flowers bloom from mid July to mid August, depending on the climate. The flowers here are grown commercially for the perfume industry.

Dried Lavender
Dried lavender has a lovely scent. It can be used in home decor, and also used to make fragrant sachets for freshening small spaces.

Lavender's Purple (Dilly Dilly)...

Mmm... Delicious!

Lavender can be added to food as a condiment. It adds a lovely fragrance and floral taste to food. Lavender is often used with meat, vegetables, baked goods, ice cream and in drinks.

Beautiful Lavender

Lavender is native to the Mediterranean region and is widely planted. Lavender blossoms are stalks with purple, blue or light purple flowers. Lavender plants are lovely and can help to beautify the surroundings. Thus, lavender is a common garden plant.

62

Purple (Dilly Dilly)...

Lavender has a wide range of commercial uses and can be made into various products such as lavender lotions, lavender incense and lavender soaps. The picture shows lavender soaps.

Butterfly
BEAUTY SHOP

LAVENDER

Lavandula angustifolia
100% Pure & Natural
Essential Oil
Net 1 fl. oz (30 mL)

Lavender essential oil is extracted from lavender plants. It can be used as a massage oil or added to bath or footbath water. The calming effects of lavender help to relax muscles and relieve fatigue and anxiety.

The Helpful Herb

Traditional Medicine

In traditional medicine and herbal practices, mugwort is valued for use in digestive and women's health. It has been used to stimulate appetite, relieve indigestion and treat menstrual problems.

Soaps and Ointments

Mugwort can be made into soaps and mugwort ointments. It is believed to be suitable for sensitive skin.

Yeeha! Yeeha!

When will I finish plucking all these?

I'm so tired!

Come on. Sow these seeds in the soil, then water them!

Granny, do you have the wugwort seeds? I want to plant some wugworts too!

Do you mean mugwort? I don't plant mugwort with seeds; I usually transplant them.

Mugwort is a strong-growing herbaceous plant. It grows rapidly through its underground root system. I'll transplant some new seedlings into a pot for you.

Vegetable Dyes
Mugwort can also be used as a dye. Making dye from natural plants, Chinese herbs, flowers, vegetables and tea is a traditional practice. These natural dyes may then be used to dye fabrics.

The Helpful Herb

The Helpful Herb

Edible and Aromatic

Mugwort is an edible herb with aromatic, bitter-tasting leaves. It is used as a flavouring in Chinese, Korean and Japanese dishes. It's also a natural colourant in making cakes.

The Mugwort

Mugwort is a herbaceous plant of the family Compositae that is widely distributed in East Asia and Europe.

Seed

A mugwort seed has a long, pointy shape and grows at temperatures ranging from 15°C to 30°C.

Seedling

A mugwort leaf blade has petioles. The leaf blade of the seedling looks like a split feather.

Dormancy

The mugwort is dormant in the winter. It only grows in the spring.

Maturity

A pointed leaf is characteristic of a mature mugwort.

The back of a mugwort leaf has fine white hair. So, the blade surface appears white.

Flowers

The mugwort blossoms between summer to early fall.

68

The Helpful Herb

Mega Mushroom

Wow! It's a huge reishi mushroom!

Hello? Chief! I've found a huge reishi mushroom. Can you send someone over to help me move it?

Okay, Mir!

One! Two! One! Two!

A while later...

70

Mega Mushroom

Mir's house...

This must be valuable...

Medicinal Mushroom

The reishi mushroom, also known as lingzhi, is a medicinal mushroom that has been used in Eastern medicine for hundreds of years. It is believed to boost the immune system and to have anti-cancer properties. Powdered forms or extracts of the mushroom are commonly used.

Wow! What's this? It's huge!

This is a reishi mushroom.

Why is it different from those I see in the market?

The ones you see in the market are usually planted artificially. But this is a wild reishi mushroom. This is the first time I've seen such a huge reishi mushroom too!

Uncle, can you give me a reishi mushroom seed?

Why?

I want to take it home and plant it in the soil!

Reishi mushrooms do not have seeds. And they grow on tree trunks or roots to obtain nutrients from the trees.

Ha ha ha!

Appearance

The reishi mushroom is kidney-shaped with a deep-red cap that lightens to yellow or orange at the edges. It has a glossy appearance and cloud-shaped rings. Spores come out from tiny pores on the underside of the mushroom.

Oh, why do they have to obtain nutrients from the trees?

Well, that's because reishi mushrooms do not have chlorophyll and cannot carry out photosynthesis to make food for themselves.

So... If they don't have seeds, how do they reproduce?

They reproduce by means of spores.

When the fruiting body of a reishi mushroom ripens, it emits spores. When the spores settle in a suitable environment, they will grow mycelia that grow into new mushrooms.

Oh, I see!

Do reishi mushrooms generally grow in forests?

Yes. They can only grow rapidly in forests with high humidity and low levels of sunlight.

A Cause of Wood Rot

Reishi mushrooms are shelf mushrooms that grow horizontally out of the trunks of dead or dying trees. They grow mycelia that invade the tree trunks or roots, causing the wood to rot and appear bleached. Reishi mushrooms generally prefer hardwood trees such as oak, elm, beech and maple.

73

Mega Mushroom

Growing Antlers
When cultivated in a closed environment, reishi mushrooms grow to become antler-shaped.

The Growth Of Reishi Mushrooms

Mega Mushroom

The reishi mushroom, or Ganoderma lucidum, belongs to a group of mushrooms called polyphore mushrooms, which form large fruiting bodies. They are bitter tasting with a pleasant smell.

Before a reishi mushroom ripens, its cap is soft and has a yellow-white tender growth ring on its edge.

When the growth ring turns reddish brown, the cap begins to become leathery (hard). It means the reishi mushroom is already ripe and should be harvested.

The shed used to artificially cultivate reishi mushrooms has to be well-ventilated, with optimal light and smooth water drainage. Hence, it is usually built in a forest or near a water source.

Fashionable in Fungi

Fashionable in Fungi

Made from Spores

Muskin, or mushroom leather, is made from fungal spores from *Phellinus ellipsoideus*, a large parasitic fungus. The material is soft, strong and has a texture like suede.

Animal-friendly Material

Muskin can grow to standard cowhide size in about 2 weeks. Producing the same size of cowhide by raising cattle would take about 2 years. No animals are killed in the production of Muskin, making it a sustainable alternative to animal leather.

Similar Materials

MYX, a material made in Denmark, is similar to Muskin. Both are organic fabrics that are made from mushrooms. The lampshade in the picture is made from Myx.

Products Made Of Muskin

Bags

Muskin can be easily made into numerous forms. Thus, it can be used to make all types of leather bags and hats.

Bracelets

Since Muskin is suitable for direct contact with human skin, it has become one of the materials favoured by bracelet manufacturers. Muskin is also suitable for making necklaces, earpieces and watch straps.

Shoes

About 20 billion pairs of shoes are produced around the world each year. However, only 5 per cent of them are recyclable. Being aware of this, Kristel Peters, a Belgian shoe designer, uses Muskin to make shoes, thus reducing the wastage of resources.

So, How Much Do You Really Know About Useful Plants and Fungi?

Challenge yourself to recall key moments of your Adventures with Useful Plants and Fungi, and find out where you rank in the Garden of Growth!

Get ready, get set, scan!

GARDEN OF GROWTH	
10	Brilliant Botanist, we're impressed!
9–8	Almost a Plant Perfectionist! Well done!
7–6	A tree-mendous effort! Keep improving!
5–4	A little of a late bloomer? Try again!
3–0	Find the root of your problems! Don't give up and try again!

Why are whale sharks endangered?
What can bamboo charcoal be used for?
Where can we find pink sand?
What are evergreen plants?
Who invented batteries?

Introducing the sensational new *World of Science* comics series designed specially for inquiring young minds! Experience Science come alive through dynamic, full-colour comics.

Books in this series so far:
- *Birds*
- *Plants and Fungi*
- *Insects*
- *Aquatic Creatures*
- *Human Body*
- *Land Animals*
- *Reptiles and Amphibians*
- *Natural Wonders*
- *How Things Work*
- *Great Minds*
- *Germs and Your Health*
- *Green Movement*
- *More Land Animals*
- *Materials*
- *Technology and Gadgets*
- *Endangered Animals*
- *More Materials*
- *More Natural Wonders*
- *Useful Plants and Fungi*
- *Discoveries and Inventions*

Look out for *Edible Plants, Earth Sciences, How More Things Work, Man-Made Marvels, Health and the Human Body,* and many more!

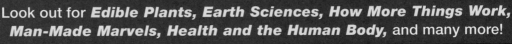